21ST Century Skills **INNOVATION LIBRARY** | **Exploring the Internet of Things**

Smart Vehicles

Martin Gitlin

Cherry Lake Press

Published in the United States of America by Cherry Lake Publishing
Ann Arbor, Michigan
www.cherrylakepublishing.com

Reading Adviser: Marla Conn, MS, Ed., Literacy specialist, Read-Ability, Inc.

Photo Credits: © metamorworks/Shutterstock, cover, 1; © blvdone/Shutterstock, 5; © Rachid Jalayanadeja/Shutterstock, 7; © Oleg Mikhaylov/Shutterstock, 8; © Kristi Blokhin/Shutterstock, 11; © jan kranendonk/Shutterstock, 13; © Ed Aldridge/Shutterstock, 15; © MikeDotta/Shutterstock, 16; © Rimba Anggara Rusli/Shutterstock, 17; © Chesky/Shutterstock, 18; © Grzegorz Czapski/Shutterstock, 21; © Arnold O. A. Pinto/Shutterstock, 23; © Yugong Luo/Shutterstock, 24; © dekitateyo/Shutterstock, 27; © flydragon/Shutterstock, 29

Graphic Element Credits: © Ohn Mar/Shutterstock.com, back cover, multiple interior pages;
© Dmitrieva Katerina/Shutterstock.com, back cover, multiple interior pages;
© advent/Shutterstock.com, back cover, front cover, multiple interior pages;
© Visual Generation/Shutterstock.com, multiple interior pages;
© anfisa focusova/Shutterstock.com, front cover, multiple interior pages;
© Babich Alexander/Shutterstock.com, back cover, front cover, multiple interior pages

Library of Congress Cataloging-in-Publication Data

Names: Gitlin, Marty, author.
Title: Smart vehicles / by Martin Gitlin.
Description: Ann Arbor, Michigan : Cherry Lake Publishing Group, 2020. | Series: Exploring the internet of things | Includes index. | Audience: Grades 4-6
Identifiers: LCCN 2020003057 (print) | LCCN 2020003058 (ebook) | ISBN 9781534168930 (hardcover) | ISBN 9781534170612 (paperback) | ISBN 9781534172456 (pdf) | ISBN 9781534174290 (ebook)
Subjects: LCSH: Automated vehicles–Juvenile literature.
Classification: LCC TL152.8 .G583 2020 (print) | LCC TL152.8 (ebook) | DDC 629.222–dc23
LC record available at https://lccn.loc.gov/2020003057
LC ebook record available at https://lccn.loc.gov/2020003058

Printed in the United States of America
Corporate Graphics

Table of Contents

Introduction

It had been the same for more than 100 years. Every car had a driver. Only in futuristic movies could one see a driverless vehicle. Times have changed. The future has become reality. Self-driving cars can be seen rolling down the roads of America. About 100,000 cars with some level of **autonomous** function could be in operation by 2022.

This is being achieved through the Internet of Things (IoT). IoT uses **sensors** to connect devices to the internet and to each other.

The advent of IoT was made possible by computer chips that were small enough to place into almost anything. The first computer chips were created in 1961 by Jack Kilby and Robert Noyce. Durable and powerful computer chips capture sounds. They sense light and temperature. And they have become cheaper to use. In 2018 alone, China spent more than $300 billion importing these small devices.

Experts believe that both IoT-connected cars and fully autonomous cars will make the roads safer for everyone, from drivers to pedestrians.

IoT **technology** had already impacted driving. It produced advantages such as **GPS** systems and smartphone connectivity. But those advances seem minor compared to the emergence of self-driving vehicles. Nearly all cars are predicted to be self-driving in 2040.

Cars are not the only vehicles to benefit. Autonomous tractors have already started saving farmers time. Connected buses will tell people at stops exactly when they will arrive. Trains will use sensors to detect problems ahead and avoid accidents. Trucks will "talk" to each other to determine the shortest routes to destinations.

IoT technology promises safer and easier travel. But only time will tell what impact it will have on the world of transportation.

CHAPTER ONE

Smart Vehicles

Imagine driving to work or school while taking a nap. Or while finishing the homework you were supposed to do the night before. Doing all this and more while behind the wheel used to be just a dream. But such dreams are coming true. Self-driving cars have arrived. They work through IoT connectivity. Sensors read radar lasers and powerful cameras. They map out the car's surroundings. Sensors send instructions to the steering, **acceleration**, and brakes. Sensors also send signals to avoid obstacles on the road. They instruct the vehicle to obey traffic rules.

Experts predict that someday in the near future, all cars will be fully autonomous. Because of this prediction, the Society of Automotive Engineers International created six standard levels of autonomous cars.

The Tesla app allows drivers to "summon" their car from up to 200 feet (60.9 meters) away!

The AAA Foundation for Traffic Safety indicates that almost 60 percent of teen accidents are caused by distracted driving. Self-driving cars could bring this number to 0.

- **Level 0: No Automation**. The driver is in control of all driving. The car doesn't have any automated assistance technologies.
- **Level 1: Driver Assistance**. The driver is in control of all driving, but the car provides basic assistance, including cruise control and automatic emergency braking.
- **Level 2: Partial Automation**. In certain situations, these cars can control the acceleration, brake, and steer on their own, but drivers must stay alert and keep their hands on the wheel.
- **Level 3: Conditional Automation**. In certain situations, these cars handle all aspects of driving. Although level 3

drivers don't need to keep their hands on the wheel, they do need to be ready to take over.

- **Level 4: High Automation**. In almost all situations, these cars handle all aspects of driving. Drivers don't need to pay too much attention, but may need to take over in the event the car is unable to drive itself.
- **Level 5: Full Automation**. These cars don't require a driver as they are capable of driving in all situations. They require no human interaction. Passengers simply enter an address and are driven there.

The age of autonomous cars has arrived. In 2018, Google's autonomous cars drove 1.2 million miles (1.9 million kilometers) in California as they were being tested. You may have spotted them; they have round black sensors built on top. But the changes might happen slowly. In 2019, 37 states in America had passed laws regarding self-driving cars.

Most cars are already **embedded** with connected devices. They predict when parts will need to be fixed. They help cars fit themselves into tight parking spaces without driver assistance. They connect to the internet to let passengers watch movies and play games. They will do more in time. Cars could receive **data** from sensor-driven streetlights and signs. They will send important information to drivers such as open parking spaces and traffic jams. Cars are the most commonly used vehicle to get an IoT makeover. But there is no limit to the variety of vehicles that will be connected. In 2018, Switzerland introduced its first self-driving bus, which is also electric.

Autonomous tractors already till the soil. They drag equipment that can plant acres. And they can make every twist and turn along the way by themselves. Many buses are connected to the internet. They receive data from traffic signals to learn the fastest route to their next stop. There are trains that use sensors that detect dangerous track conditions. This helps reduce the chance of accidents. In the future, trucks might get alerts about weather conditions hundreds of miles ahead. That will allow drivers to decide the ideal time to stop for the night. Ambulances could turn red lights green. That will help them get sick people to the hospital faster.

IoT technology promises to forever alter the world of transportation. But with any technology revolution, there are problems. Those problems must be solved for IoT to best serve people and their vehicles.

Companies are releasing driverless scooters that can return to the closest charging station or "drive" to people in search of a scooter.

AVOIDING TRAIN ACCIDENTS

Many people were severely injured or killed when a train derailed in Pennsylvania in 2015. It was a case of human error. That is the case in about 40 percent of all train accidents. The train was simply moving too fast.

The accident could have been avoided. That area of track could have been fitted with what is called Positive Train Control (PTC). PTC is a complex and predictive system. It monitors train speed and location. It informs signaling equipment that the train is arriving. And it then controls the train's speed. This eliminates human error.

The sensor system is expensive. It only prevents certain types of accidents. It cannot stop trains at crossings with cars or people on the tracks. But it can save lives.

Adding IoT sensors to train tracks would also help reduce the number of delays.

CHAPTER TWO

Benefits and Drawbacks

About 40,000 people were killed in car crashes in the United States in 2018. And about 4.5 million were seriously injured. Those were about the same numbers as in 2016 and 2017. IoT technology in vehicles, commonly referred to as an automated driving system, can help. Research shows that autonomous vehicles will cause fewer and less severe accidents. That would mean safer passengers, bicyclists, and pedestrians.

That same research proves that IoT has already made a difference. Sensors used in collision-avoiding systems have forced cars to steer away and brake when a dangerous situation arises. Stability control systems also help drivers stay steady on sharp turns and slippery roads. Drivers can quickly select which wheel to use for braking. Studies indicate that has saved thousands of lives. The U.S. Department of Transportation has estimated that IoT technology in vehicles could reduce fatal accidents by 94 percent!

In 2014, Tesla introduced the Model S. It was the first model with autopilot.

Autonomous cars could eliminate city parking spaces and garages. These spaces could be repurposed into public parks or community gardens.

Car owners are not the only people who have benefited from IoT technology. It has also made a positive impact on many others. Farmers get work done or simply relax while their connected tractors till the fields. Bus drivers and commuters benefit from data that predict precise arrival times. Train passengers feel safer because of sensors that detect danger ahead.

But there could also be danger ahead for IoT-connected vehicles. The technology must be made **foolproof**. Cars, trucks, and other vehicles are far too dangerous to risk safety concerns. In 2018, a self-driving car provided a deadly example. An autonomous **Uber** vehicle struck and killed a woman in

Fully autonomous cars are electric. This means they aren't adding to pollution, unlike fuel-dependent cars.

IoT-connected cars can predict when a car part will fail well before it fails. This predictive technology can help eliminate costly maintenance.

Arizona. Sensors detected no crosswalk, so the car kept moving. It did not recognize the jaywalker. The car was not fully autonomous. The driver could have taken control of the wheel. But the police investigation determined that the driver was not paying attention. She was busy streaming a television show.

Uber quickly modified its system to recognize jaywalkers. Strong **oversight** will be required to make self-driving vehicles completely safe. It is hoped that accidents won't be needed as motivation to continue that work.

Another issue is connectivity. IoT vehicles must constantly send and receive data about concerns such as traffic, **preventive** maintenance, and tracking.

The goal of IoT technology in vehicles is to create a system in which the advantages of ease and safety outweigh the concerns. That will be the task of connected car **manufacturers** moving forward.

There are several ways data is shared in IoT-connected cars:

Vehicle to infrastructure (V2I): The driver is notified by the car about the surrounding environment, including traffic and construction zones.

Vehicle to vehicle (V2V): Cars exchange data with each other. This information includes their direction, speed, and location.

Vehicle to cloud (V2C): The car sends information to be evaluated by a company via the **cloud**. This would help with preventing or diagnosing software or mechanical issues.

Vehicle to pedestrian (V2P): The car detects and notifies other cars about nearby pedestrians. The V2P system also has the ability to notify pedestrians about cars in the area.

Vehicle to everything (V2X): This data-sharing system encompasses everything from V2I to V2P.

ROLLING ALONG WITH IOT

Trucks carry a huge load around the world. They are more responsible for hauling goods from manufacturers to stores than any vehicle. About 70 percent of all cargo in the United States is carried by trucks.

They must be efficient in their jobs. That is why more trucking companies have embraced IoT technology.

Sensors allow trucking companies to track, monitor, and analyze their vehicles in real time. One example is sensors that detect low tire pressure. They send alerts that could prevent a blowout on a busy highway. IoT data will also allow truck owners to recognize needed improvements. Sensors will alert them if truck parts are dying faster than they should. Purchasing longer-lasting parts would save companies thousands of dollars in the long run.

Data will also compare routes of several drivers. It will identify which driver conserved more fuel or arrived at a destination faster. That will allow companies to create standard routes that work best.

IHS Automotive estimates that there will be 4.5 million IoT vehicles of all types in the United States by 2035.

CHAPTER THREE

The Future of IoT Vehicles

There is one basic fact about the future of connected vehicles: they are sure to gain popularity. That is especially true for self-driving cars. *Fortune* magazine predicts that only about 1 in 20 new vehicles sold in 2040 will need hands behind the wheel.

The result will be that some cars will have no passengers. They will simply be programmed to travel from one point to another. Autonomous cars and trucks will be used to deliver cargo. Or they will be used to pick people up.

A major drawback to the **influx** of self-driving vehicles could be loss of jobs. Cab and ridesharing companies such as Uber and Lyft might not employ drivers. Even bus and truck drivers could be replaced in a driverless world of transportation. In 2019, the U.S. Census Bureau reported that there were about 3.5 million truck drivers in the United States. Self-driving trucks could put these drivers out of a job.

In order to keep up with customer demand, FedEx unveiled a driverless delivery robot in early 2019: the FedEx SameDay Bot.

IoT-connected cars that aren't driverless can still reduce pollution and be personalized. For instance, Sony's Vision-S concept car could potentially detect a sleeping passenger and adjust the temperature around that seat.

Still, the advantages for drivers of semi-autonomous vehicles and passengers of self-driving cars will be many. IoT technology can create the ideal temperature inside the vehicle based on outside conditions. It could tint windows to prevent sun glare. It could even adjust lighting to fit the mood of music playing on a satellite radio station.

Sensors will weave cars through heavy traffic with no human help. The cars will embark on the fastest routes based on road and traffic conditions ahead. Their speed and steering will adjust to those conditions.

Vehicles will communicate with each other. They will receive data from connected devices such as traffic lights, stop signs, and parking meters.

And passengers can do whatever they want. They can text. They can schedule meetings while their cars **navigate** the route to work or home. They can read books or watch movies. Some will take naps if they did not get enough sleep the night before.

The success of IoT vehicles as they take over the market will be based on safety. The free time they allow passengers will mean little if they prove to be unsafe. No amount of convenience can outweigh the horror of lost lives.

That is the difference between IoT in vehicles and in other devices. Cars, trucks, trains, and buses can be dangerous. The most crucial goal of its technology is to make them safer. Nothing else compares in importance.

MIND READER

The future of IoT could include what is known as brain-to-vehicle (B2V) technology. That is the ability of a device to know what the driver wants based on brain wave activity. Those thoughts are analyzed by autonomous vehicle systems. Those systems are then used to anticipate driver behavior.

The technology is quite advanced. It is also not for every driver. It requires that drivers wear a headset with electrodes that press directly or close to their scalps. That could be uncomfortable. Yet it could help drivers avoid accidents caused by abrupt lane changes and other unsafe moves behind the wheel. But the widespread use of B2V technology seems to be far into the future.

This technology, also called brain-to-vehicle (B2V), was first introduced by car maker Nissan in 2018.

Critical Thinking and Problem Solving

The biggest problem with autonomous vehicles centers on the human factor. Those who drive for a living could be out of a job. That is certainly the fear for bus, cab, and truck drivers. Drivers of rideshare vehicles, like Uber or Lyft, are also threatened with unemployment.

What will happen to those drivers has not been determined. Perhaps companies will train professional drivers for other lines of work in the transportation industry.

Companies would save significant money as they no longer would need to pay drivers. But it will be argued that drivers' employment is more important to society than the money saved by businesses.

Think About It

Should laws be passed that don't allow professional drivers to be fired to make room for autonomous vehicles? Why or why not? What possible solutions can you come up with?

The future of IoT-connected and driverless cars is exciting, but like with any revolution, there will be resistance. Why do you think this is?

Learn More

Books

Sonnad, Haydn. *Self-Driving Cars*. Ann Arbor, MI: Cherry Lake Publishing, 2019.

Zuchora-Walske, Christine. *Self-Driving Cars*. Minneapolis, MN: ABDO Publishing, 2018.

Websites

Beanz—What Is the Internet of Things?
https://www.kidscodecs.com/what-is-internet-of-things
Discover more about IoT technology.

Wonderopolis—Can a Car Drive Itself?
https://www.wonderopolis.org/wonder/can-a-car-drive-itself
Learn more about the benefits and potential drawbacks of self-driving cars.

Glossary

acceleration (ak-sel-uh-RAY-shuhn) picking up speed in a car by putting weight on the gas pedal

autonomous (aw-TAH-nuh-muhs) working without human help

cloud (KLOUD) data that is stored on the internet

data (DAY-tuh) facts to be used for planning or making decisions

embedded (em-BED-id) set solidly in another object

foolproof (FOOL-proof) planned or done so it cannot fail

GPS (JEE PEE ES) a system that uses satellite signals to determine a user's location and give directions; stands for global positioning system

influx (IN-fluks) the arrival of a large amount of something

manufacturers (man-yuh-FAKchur-urz) companies that make things in large amounts, such as in a factory

navigate (NAV-ih-gate) to travel through a path

oversight (OH-vur-site) the responsibility for seeing that something is done correctly

preventive (prih-VEN-tiv) measures taken to prevent a negative outcome

sensors (SEN-surz) detection devices that respond by transmitting a signal

technology (tek-NAH-luh-jee) related to applying knowledge about science and industry

Uber (OO-bur) a rideshare company that transports passengers

Index